M000198829

Pure Dzogchen

Zhang Zhung Tradition

Dedication

This book is
offered to all
my kind, wise teachers
in great appreciation
of their tireless guidance.
It is dedicated to the
benefit and liberation
of my students,
and to all sentient beings.

Pure Dzogchen

Zhang Zhung Tradition

Geshe Dangsong Namgyal

Namkha Publications
California, USA

PURE DZOGCHEN
A Namkha Publications book

All Rights Reserved
Copyright © 2019 by Geshe Dangsong Namgyal

Published by Namkha Publications
P.O. Box 65, Freedom CA 95019 USA
email: namkha2018@yahoo.com

Second Edition
ISBN: 978-0-9996898-1-3 (black and white interior, Ingram)

© Traditional art line drawings created by Norbu Lhundrub.

Library of Congress Control Number: 2019916318

Contents

Introduction

I would like to share my story with you regarding how I entered the path of Pure Dzogchen. When I was young, I met the great Dzogchen masters Togden Sherab Phuntsog, Khanpo Nyima Lodo, and Lobpon Tsultrim Namdag and received Dzogchen teachings in Tibet. I had completed the nine hundred thousand round Ngondro practice and especially the Kalung Gyatso (extensive three year Ngondro).

Many Dzogchen masters said that in order to achieve perfect Dzogchen realization, it would also be good to learn about other vehicles. I followed that advice by starting in Lungkar monastery in Tibet, studying Sutra philosophy, logic, and Buddhist psychology. Most of my additional training occurred after I came to India, studying for some years at Menri Monastery, then at Sera Je monastic university with the great master Choden Rinpoche, the previous Abbot Losang Tsering, and previous Abbot Losang Delek. While at Sera Je, about three thousand monks would gather together to debate every evening and sometimes in the morning too. At those times we would recite the Heart Sutra and the Tara prayer for long spans of time. I attempted to practice Dzogchen meditation during those prayer periods. It was difficult for me to do that at first, but it became easier over time. Usually when I felt sad, homesick, angry and unhappy, I used the Dzogchen meditation, as it was tremendously helpful.

After many years, when I returned to my home lineage via Triten Norbutse Monastery in Kathmandu, Nepal, many of my friends thought I was no longer interested in Dzogchen, because I had studied so many years in Sera Monastery, where they do not practice Dzogchen. My friends presumed that I had embraced the gradual view of the Gelugpas. In fact, no one can truly assess what another's practice and view is, as that is ultimately a inner, "secret" matter, so there was no reason to try to explain my inner experience. I studied Dzogchen and Tantra with Lopon Tenzin Namdag Rinpoche in Nepal. I have studied Sutra and Tantra in depth in the Bon and Gelug traditions. In the end, I realized I was more interested in the Pure Dzogchen. So now, when I teach Dzogchen, I do not mix it with Sutra and Tantra.

This book, therefore, is a compilation of the Pure Dzogchen teachings that I have offered recently to my students and the general public in Northern California. It contains quotations from the *Oral Transmission of Zhang Zhung*.

This teaching can directly impart an experience of Nature of Mind from the beginning. It is often assumed that the path to liberation is very long, perhaps many lifetimes. In the Pure Dzogchen approach, because the Nature of Mind is communicated directly through the lineage and teacher, the process can be much faster. In Sutra teachings, the path is actually said to take three countless eons to accomplish; in Tantra, the path can be quicker, but will still involve great effort and complexities. In this Pure Dzogchen approach, because the Nature of Mind is revealed directly, its full realization can occur very quickly. As the Nature of Mind is directly accessible in Dzogchen, the process of purification occurs through the illumination arising from this revelation. The mental afflictions lose their grip on the mind as the deeper nature becomes more clear. So no matter what one's background country, gender, age, race, beliefs or history of painful experiences and emotions, the Pure Dzogchen path can swiftly bring one to the transcendent recognition of Nature of Mind with much less effort than traditional Sutra and Tantra approaches. This is because the power of this recognition directly undermines the basis of the mental afflictions, i.e. the ordinary dualistic mind.

From this perspective, meditation on the Nature of Mind is the most powerful way to purify the mind of even eons of negative karmic patterns. Because the Pure Dzogchen path is about direct experience of the Nature of Mind, study of the Buddhist Sutra and texts is not necessary. In fact, if one approaches this from a secular, agnostic, or atheist point of view, it does not matter if one studies the texts. The Nature of Mind is beyond all belief and philosophies; its reality becomes directly self-evident. The point of view of Pure Dzogchen, as a methodology can be explained philosophically, with logic and reason, even though its ultimate goal is beyond logic and reason.

In Pure Dzogchen teachings, because the Dharmakaya is always already present as the most subtle stratum of consciousness, its recognition through this teaching and practice simultaneously gives rise to Ground, Path and Result. This means that the Pure Dzogchen process, or "Path" of recognizing the ultimate Nature of Mind, or "Ground" itself, generates an ever-increasing clarity of this recognition, or "Result". Because the Pure Dzogchen posits the Nature of Mind as an inherent quality rather than a "seed" to be cultivated over time, it isn't really compatible with other approaches. The ultimate fruition of Pure Dzogchen practice is the attainment of the Rainbow Body of Light, a manifestation of deep realization unique to the Dzogchen path.

I believe that by directly introducing the primordial Buddha Nature through the Pure Dzogchen teachings, those receiving these teachings can enter into that recognition and discover true peace, strength, and fearlessness in life; and confidence in an eventual, positive death, Bardo, and rebirth experience.

Geshe Dangsong Namgyal

No. 1

Natural mind
is like a jewel.
If you're looking for mind,
you can't find it.
Even if you don't
look for it,
it is never lost
and never separate.

Looking for Mind

It is very important to recognize our mind, because through our mind we get beyond mind. Of course we all know we have mind because we are thinking all the time. What is mind? Scientists assert that mind is found in brain cells, but experience tells us that our mind and thoughts are not cells. If we actually look for the mind, it is not that easy. There are stories of students looking for their mind in the mountains or by the sea, in stones or trees. These stories point to the fact that we must look inside ourselves, not outside, to find our mind. We have our conventional mind that engages in thoughts of past, present and future. All activities are carried out by this mind but we don't know its actual condition. First we must recognize our conventional mind. After we do this, we search for our Natural Mind which is beyond the conceptions of our conventional mind and is beyond words.

No. 2

A person,
fearing birth and death,
goes into delightful
solitary retreat
in a hermitage.
That person recognizes
the base of all,
and so gains deep certainty
in innate self-awareness.

Everything Is Mind

What is our mind condition? Mind is the source of everything. All the positive and negative things we experience are dependent on mind. When we use our mind skillfully, we can have some control. For example, the practitioner who gets up in the morning and sets the motivation, "Today I want to have positive, peaceful compassion," will notice their day becomes like that. At mid-day they reflect again on their motivation. More positive thinking in the afternoon leads to good motivation into the night. Then, reflecting on those positive things that happened that day, they think, "Tomorrow I will remember that motivation again." Mind is like a king who rules over actions of body and speech like they are his servants.

Natural Mind meditation is without object. We don't try to visualize anything or focus on a chosen object. We sit with a straight back and relax our body and mind and we don't worry about thoughts that come. We just leave them be. Thoughts are mind, and we have many minds the same as we have many thoughts. We don't make any effort and we don't try to stop thoughts. Natural Mind is recognized when we relax and don't try to make anything happen. We just stay natural. It's ok if we can do this for 5 minutes or even 1 minute! Just return to the meditation if you find your mind has wandered. It's best to stop meditation while we are having a good experience, and come back later.

No. 3

Natural Mind's
positive qualities
are inconceivable,
like revealing
a king's treasure.
The one who rests
within its true meaning
enjoys the inexhaustible
wealth of its fruition.

Two Processes at the Beginning

Calm Abiding means being able to rest your mind without distraction while focusing on an imagined object until you can imagine it as a clear, bright and heavy-looking image in your mind. Imagine the object about an inch tall and in front of you about an arm's length away. Just keep practicing and you will get some experience. You will get some benefit even from achieving early stages of the practice. We do this as a preliminary to our main meditation practice. We can try to decrease the obstacles of dull sleepiness or busy agitation.

Natural Mind Meditation is our main meditation practice. To start, we analyze: "Where is my mind?" Can we really find it in the body somewhere? Observe the thoughts as they come. Where do they come from? Where do they go? We have conceptions, misconceptions and thoughts coming and going in our minds. Notice what thoughts come and see them without judgment, then watch as they disappear.

Meditation on Natural Mind solves the problems of dull sleepiness or busy agitation in the mind when we simply recognize how these obstacles come and then go.

21

No. 4

The mind and
all mental states
dissolve into the space
of the nature of mind.
All activities dissolve
into the space of stillness.
All forms of speech dissolve
into the space of silence.
All the clouds of thoughts
and recollections
dissolve into the
space free of thought.

Recognizing the Natural Mind

Normally we haven't paid attention to the mind at all and haven't had any insight into what is happening. Now, as we begin to notice how thoughts come and go, we see that the mind is constantly busy. Meditation gradually reduces that busyness. But how do we know when we have recognized the Natural Mind? There are analogies for signs we may notice as our meditation improves and we begin to have control of the mind:

- It is like a bee that never travels far from the flower.

- It stays just like a fish stays in the water.

- Like an ocean without wind, the mind is calm.

- Like a mountain, the mind is stable.

These examples illustrate the happy, meditating mind relaxes and doesn't need to follow many thoughts. The meditator finds that just enjoying the experience of Natural Mind is enough and there isn't a lot of engagement with many different thoughts going here and there.

No. 5

The first Buddha
is self-originated,
primordial purity...
in essence, the Natural Mind.
Everything is included in
Natural Mind,
without separation.

Primordial Purity

It is said that samsara and nirvana both come from the primordial purity of the Natural Mind. What can we understand from this? If we consider that "samsara" is like the life we have, where we continually experience our ups and downs, and then contrast that with the lasting peace and happiness that is "nirvana," we may ask ourselves how they can come from the same source? We all have good and bad karma. Things go well for us and then something happens and we feel unhappy. The uninterrupted peace of nirvana, free from uncontrolled karma, is the opposite, so in what way can we say they are the same? We can see that both samsara and nirvana are states of mind. Happiness, suffering and peace are mind-based. Everything is included in Natural Mind. We always have the primordially pure Natural Mind. Everything in our experience is an expression of it. Knowing this, we can control our minds.

No. 6

The Natural Mind is self-originated and
is the three bodies of Buddha.
The single sphere has spontaneity
and is a marvelous thing!

Spontaneous Qualities of Natural Mind

The Natural Mind has a spontaneous quality. "Spontaneous" in Dzogchen means unobstructed potentiality.

The Natural Mind has spontaneous enlightened body, wisdom, path and result. Whoever attains good realization has the five delusions liberated. The five delusions arise as anger, attachment, ignorance, pride and jealousy.

The unobstructed six perfections of generosity, patience, morality, effort, concentration, and discriminating knowledge are manifested. For example, the Natural Mind is freedom from miserliness. It is the unobstructed potential for generosity. Natural Mind is beyond the vows and promises of samaya and is the unobstructed potential for morality.

The five delusions are liberated because Natural Mind is the unobstructed potential of the five wisdoms.

According to the lower schools of Buddhism, there are eight different levels of view, conduct, result and best quality; these also spontaneously arise in Natural Mind.

27

No. 7

All that appears and exists,
samsara and nirvana,
everything is included
in ultimate bodhicitta—
for this purpose,
great perfection.

What is Great Perfection (Dzog Chen)?

Three things: ground, path, and result, are at once included in the nature of awareness in perfect fulfillment. According to Dzogchen or the Great Perfection, practitioners doing practices either attain Dzogchen or not.

There are four possible configurations: 1) one who has realization without understanding the teaching; it is great, but not perfection. 2) one who has understood the teaching without realization appearing; it is perfection, but not great. 3) one who has realization appear with understanding; it is absolutely great perfection. 4) one who has neither attained realization, nor is Dzogchen understood; it is not great or perfection.

All sentient beings have self-originated wisdom. Therefore, someone could possibly attain appeared realization before getting the Dzogchen teaching. Realization such as this is great, but not perfection. Someone could receive the teaching, but not have realization appear because they have not practiced enough.

What does perfection mean? All conceptual terminologies are integrated into one essence of meaning. The qualities of all the vehicles include the qualities of the natural state. All mental constructs pacify into the basic foundation. All words pacifying into the basic foundation is beyond words. Why does this become great? Because it is free from any limits, free from any bounds. It is not equalled by any other quality. It is unexcelled; therefore, the teaching is called great.

No. 8

You look for
the very subtle
meaning.
If you look for it
you won't see it.
Without seeing
is the best seeing.

Qualities of Natural Mind

Four Inconceivable Qualities:

- Passed beyond View
- Passed beyond Meditation
- Passed beyond Action
- Passed beyond Result

Natural Mind is beyond mind, like space on a moonless, cloudless night. One can't conceive of just how vast it is. It is without end, or measurement. We can scarcely imagine its depth. Who at some time has not been awed by the inconceivable vastness of space?

The higher practitioner's experience is like this. The meditator passes beyond mind and experiences the inconceivable vastness of the Natural Mind.

Finally they decide, "It is like this." This is the final ultimate truth. It is the ultimate: beyond mind, beyond speech and inconceivable.

No. 9

Because the door to the
treasure of the mind is opened,
Everything you need is complete within you.

Realizing Our Good Quality

Now we are thinking, "I want to meditate." What are our aspirations? We all have a good, important quality, Natural Mind, but we don't recognize it. If we don't know it, it can't help us. At present, we are always following thoughts that arise in our minds. This leads to the discontent and the negativity that we experience. We may be wishing for something better. Usually, we don't believe we have the same quality as holy beings. We can easily get disheartened and so we don't put effort toward higher level meditation. Why do we feel discouraged? It is because we don't know that we already have this good quality. It may seem like the good quality of Buddha nature or Godliness is very far away. That's due to not knowing that we already have the good quality now. We want to attain realization of our good quality. We already have Natural Mind. We need to believe that, to realize it and to remember that at all times.

We can get some experience through our meditation. When we recognize our Natural Mind, we understand the quality that we already have and we never want to be separate from it. Our mind becomes very rich. We are encouraged and we get energy, strength, and a powerful mind.

No. 10

The practitioners are enlightened
and at that time, defiling aggregates
never come again. They have achieved
the great transformation
of the Rainbow Body.
They work for the benefit of sentient beings
like the reflection of the moon in water.

What is Rainbow Body?

Many Dzogchen practitioners have achieved Rainbow Body. For some of them, the body dissolves into space with rainbows and lights. For others the body becomes smaller in a few days and they are surrounded by light. Finally the hair and nails are all that is left. The body disappears like salt dissolving in water. Then for others, after death, a rainbow appears in the sky, or light or special clouds. The body is still there but is much smaller.

Why do some Dzogchen practitioners accomplish Rainbow Body? There are three phenomena that disappear into innate awareness: Outer, Inner and Secret.

Outer phenomena are the grosser consciousnesses associated with the senses along with the delusions of mental consciousness. Inner phenomena are the more subtle thoughts and conceptions. Secret phenomena are the manifestations of luminosity. These three disappear into innate awareness. At that time the luminosity of the body, forms, light and mandalas all dissolve into awareness like a cloud disappears into the sky.

The Rainbow Body is a sign of the practice and experience of the person. They have achieved complete primordial awareness. They always stay in that awareness. This level is called "enlightenment."

No. 11

Seeing the delusions
as faults is grasping.
Just leave them,
that is the method.
Liberate them into space.

"Without Hope or Fear" Is the Fruition

If you were to imagine going to a golden place, everything there would be golden. Like this, imagine reaching a higher experience of Natural Mind meditation. All appearances and phenomena are included in Natural Mind, not separate. Having reached the highest state of meditation, there is no need for hope in achieving further qualities. You don't need anything more. There is no samsara, no hell realm and no suffering and so there is no need for fear. There is no longer any object of fear.

The fruition is the enlightenment of a Buddha, and then, at this time, you can use the three bodies. Your self-cognition is the Dharmakaya, your body-mind connection is the Sambhogakaya and your activities are the Nirmanakaya. These are manifestations to benefit all sentient beings. There is no hope or fear in the higher states.

No. 12

The light appears
clearly in the sky.
Self originated sound
comes from emptiness.
Form is inseparable
from emptiness and clear light.
It is called objects of appearance.

Three Appearances

The three appearances–luminous color, sound and form–are manifestations of awareness wisdom. Color comes from the clarity quality of awareness. It is similar to a rainbow. Sound comes from emptiness awareness and it is similar to an echo. Form is from inseparable emptiness and clarity awareness and it is like a reflection.

Awareness is the source of the five colors–red, yellow, white, green and blue. The five great wisdoms come from color and are actually not separate from them. The five delusions of sentient beings also appear from the five colors. Just like a mirror, everything can appear. Good things and bad things appear in the mirror but the mirror itself is not disturbed. Positive and negative are no obstruction.

As the higher practitioner analyzes the Mother, Son and Appearances, the Five Great Wisdoms appear. Everything becomes positive. All that appears is Natural Mind and manifests from the Natural Mind as positive qualities, pure land or mandala because Mother, Son and Appearance are inseparable.

No. 13

Co-emergent ignorance
is the main source.
Conceptual ignorance is
the conditioned source.
The fruition is the five delusions.
These are the causes
of circling in samsara.

How Ignorance and Samsara Arise

The lion sees his face in the water. He thinks there's another lion there, but there isn't. Even his face is not there in the reflection. Like this, we have the three subtle appearances–color, form and sound–that are manifestations of Natural Mind.

At the beginning, we have only Primordial Purity. Later on, we get co-emergent ignorance. Just as the lion thinks there's another lion in water, we see the three appearances. But then we grasp at them as coming from something other than our own Natural Mind. Co-emergent ignorance causes conception which grasps at form, smell, taste, sounds, and touch and the five objects of these senses. At the same time conceptual ignorance arises which grasps at "I" and "you." Then the five delusions arise from that ignorance. Conceptual ignorance is like a strong wind that causes the clouds to move quickly. The five delusions come and they create Karma. The karmic results are the three realms and six categories of beings.

From anger comes the form realm.
From attachment comes the desire realm.

From six habitual delusions come the six categories of beings and the Twelve Links. This condition is called Samsara.

No. 14

Emptiness quality
is Dharmakaya.
Clarity quality
is Sambhogakaya.
Variety of miraculous
ability is Nirmanakaya.

Three Enlightened Bodies According to Dzogchen

The three enlightened bodies are the Dharmakaya, Sambhogakaya and the Nirmanakaya. These are three qualities of Natural Mind. In Dzogchen teachings, one method of introducing these is through talking about their location and then describing what each is.

Since you can't point to a particular thing that is Dharmakaya, which is vast and sky-like, its location is described as being "located" in the quality of primordial purity of self-awareness with no object or subject. It is without partiality and is primordial purity.

The Sambhogakaya is located in our heart. In the Tibetan tradition, the mind is located in the heart. The object is awareness with three manifestations: form, color and sound. Every phenomena is spontaneous there.

The Nirmanakaya is located in the path of the three channels. The awareness that appears is the six phenomena and six objects appearing through the six consciousnesses. Actually, these are the enlightened body and Buddha field. Because we have delusions, we don't recognize that we already have these, and samsara comes. These bodies are spontaneously included in Natural Mind.

No. 15

To maintain awareness
is the natural condition.
Whatever comes,
the mind doesn't
follow that object.
At that time,
the practitioner
achieves independence.

Appear and Liberate Simultaneously

If the child is lost, the mother will look for him or her until found, even if she must look for a long time. Like this, all appearances manifest from and return to Natural Mind. If we have good realization, all phenomena just disappear into the basic, space-like Natural Mind. This realization is called liberation. To the realized, highest practitioner, whatever they see is enlightened body, speech, and mind, and all Buddha activities are mandala and pure land appearances. This is liberation. Then also, when the beginning practitioner, for example, has negative thoughts, they watch them dissolve into Natural Mind. This is also called liberation. The practice, then, is called "Appearance and Liberation at the Same Time." We try to practice this in meditation and in our daily lives.

For the beginning practitioner, the result and the source look like different things, but in fact, the result is part of the source. If we have realization that they are the same, they appear and are liberated at the same time.

No. 16

The example is space
The sign is great emptiness
The meaning is ultimate truth.

Three Ways to Understand Natural Mind

Three ways to understand Natural Mind are through:

Example: An illustration that is easy to understand and everyone knows and sees—a metaphor.

Sign: The deeper meaning to which the metaphor points.

Meaning: What is essential to understand.

In regards to Natural Mind:

The example is space. In space there is a rainbow, clouds and many other things. These appear, stay and disappear in space. Space has no end, color, or partiality. Natural Mind is like space; thoughts and delusions appear, stay and disappear into it.

The sign is the clarity quality, the emptiness quality and the great quality which is the union of clarity and emptiness. What is appearance to mind and mental factors comes and goes without grasping because Natural Mind is without grasping.

The meaning is ultimate truth which is non-arising. There is appearance of phenomena and entities but all that appears stays within ultimate truth and disappears into ultimate truth. There is no partiality; it is beyond speech and beyond conception.

The meaning is single-pointed ultimate truth.

No. 17

What is
awareness wisdom?
Its essence is
clear light.
It is natural,
without
consciousness
and conception.

Recognizing Mother, Child and Manifestation

For the Dzogchen meditator, it is important to recognize the connection between aspects of realization, like Mother, Child and Manifestation.

Mother is primordial purity and is like the sky. It is the foundation of samsara, nirvana, Buddha and sentient beings. It is the great source.

Child is awareness wisdom and is like the sunshine in the sky. You stay on this unobstructed, naked awareness without grasping and without effort.

Manifestation is appearances and these come from the awareness wisdom. Form, sound and color are the most subtle appearances.

It's very important to recognize Mother, Child and Manifestation in meditation and get realizations of these. But this practice is also very important for daily life. If you have good realization, then many sufferings and problems are solved. When you get a problem, these are very helpful.

No. 18

There is an object
but that object is
without foundation.
The appearance is nominal.
The name is the same
as the appearance.
The name has no foundation.

Karma and Natural Mind

Negative karma is the main source of suffering for sentient beings. How is karma created? Through the six consciousnesses, we grasp at the six objects. For example, if you see a flower, the eye consciousness causes the arising of the mental consciousness (or thought), which in turn grasps onto it as an object. We are presently controlled by this grasping and so then we create the karma that results. From this, we circle in samsara.

What causes this circle of samsara? It is from not having realized Natural Mind. If we have a good level of realization, then when consciousness grasps at an object, we just watch it. We can see that the foundation of that consciousness looks like the sky and the consciousness itself looks like a rainbow appearing there. The foundation is actually the Natural Mind. The practitioner's appearances and actions of consciousness are the Nirmanakaya mandala. The mandala is the Buddha and the Buddha land.

Therefore there is no negative and no bad karma. It is like a painting of an apple tree on the wall. We see the apple there but we cannot eat it. It is only an appearance and not truly there.

No. 19

Defilement disappears
into non-defilement,
like salt dissolves
in water—
bad karma and
all delusions
are liberated
into the natural state.

Purification in Dzogchen

Over the course of uncountable rebirths, we have accumulated bad karma, "stored" in habitual tendencies. These karmic seeds easily trigger suffering and rebirth in the "twirling" of dependent origination. However, all bad karma can be purified through the method of the four opponent powers. This is the case in Sutra, Tantra, and all Buddhist traditions, including Dzogchen. In Dzogchen, purification is a matter of the realization of the Nature of Mind, and good experience in that meditation. In this view, all bad karma and non-virtues are realized as being without foundation. All seeds of karma are sealed into the Nature of Mind, meaning that they are the manifestation of Nature of Mind.

Through this realization, all karma is "purified" in that it was not created in the first place. For example, you can't paint on space. Even if colors arise, there is no canvas upon which they can be fixed. Phenomena are without any other foundation. The only foundation is the Natural State. According to the teaching, meditating for one second on this nature of mind purifies eons of bad karma. Therefore, this is the best method for purification.

No. 20

Five delusions are
completely purified.
Primordial awareness
is naturally abiding
in five wisdoms.

Introducing Secret Refuge

Dharma teaching says that refuge practice is important. Why do we need refuge practice? We know that we, and all sentient beings have troubles and suffering, and we look for help. We have both gross and subtle suffering in Samsara.

If we recognize Natural Mind and gain experience, then it helps relieve our suffering—even the root of suffering. All suffering comes from temporary phenomena. Higher realization brings control over bad appearances and one gains mastery over all phenomena.

When we recognize Natural Mind and believe in it, that is refuge practice. When we have higher experience, then Nirvana and all Buddha's qualities are automatically achieved. At that time, many enlightened qualities manifest –such as the five wisdoms.

Intrinsic awareness is the special mind of all the Buddhas. The teaching says that when we see self-knowing wisdom, we see thousands of Buddha faces.

When we practice, the gross and subtle suffering is liberated into Natural Mind. We are protected from suffering. This is the best refuge practice.

No. 21

Bodhicitta is
non-duality
and primordially
without effort.
When we understand
the King of Awareness,
Bodhicitta, it is like the
luminous, vast sky.
It is all-pervasive
luminosity
without restriction.
It is called Bodhicitta.

Two Bodhicittas in Dzogchen

Dzogchen tradition is a Mahayana tradition, therefore we practice not just for ourselves, but also so for all sentient beings to become enlightened. Reducing selfishness is the foundation of practice. All of the Sutra teachings that explain relative Bodhicitta and Compassion are no different from Dzogchen.

Two Bodhicittas are included in the Mahayana mind training traditions. They are Conventional or Relative Bodhicitta and Ultimate or Self-knowing Bodhicitta.

In Tibetan, *"jangchub sem"* is Bodhicitta. *Jang* means that primordially all ignorance, delusion and faults are purified. *Chub* means all enlightened qualities are included in the spontaneous achievement of the highest realization. *Sem* means the Natural state of mind; therefore in Dzogchen, it is the Ultimate Bodhicitta.

When we practice, all sentient beings appear and are sealed or included within the Natural Mind. Because of the Mahayana motivation, this practice brings about the enlightenment of all sentient beings.

All phenomena are sealed into Natural Mind. This is the best meaning for bringing all sentient beings to enlightenment. It is the best Bodhicitta practice.

No. 22

Look, everything
is a case of
self-origination.
All the phenomena
of our experience
doesn't come from outside;
all originates
from Natural Mind.

Thoughts Passing Like Clouds

Imagine a space-like expanse that opens infinitely in all directions. In that sky-like space, clouds appear and then, by themselves, they disappear. No effort is required. Airplanes come and go, black clouds and birds come and go, while the deep unchanging space remains free and pure. Like this, our mind is primordially pure. Like this, thoughts, fear, worries, happiness, suffering and joy all appear in our mind and, by themselves, they come and then go in the expanse of the Natural Mind.

What would it be like if we experienced a thought as a cloud that is passing through now, without seeing it as good or bad and without getting lost in it, without following it?

Natural mind meditation is like this. If we are trying to stop the thought, that is not the meditation. If we are following, or getting lost in the thought, this also is not meditation. Just leaving the mind be natural, letting the thought come and go is the meditation. When we have realization of this, we are no longer controlled by our thoughts.

No. 23

The mistake
is attachment
to the meditation
experience.
The meditator's
calm state
is very present.
It looks like a
traveller asleep
on the road.

Three Steps: Rest, Destroy, Remain

In the beginning, we meditate without focusing on an object—form, color, smell, visualization, etc. The three steps to use at this time are: rest, destroy and remain.

Rest: We should meditate without following concepts. We rest on the impossibility of apprehension. Our meditation is relaxed, resting free and easy. Leave it as it naturally is.

Destroy: During meditation, when a problem arises, destroy it. We might find that the mind has started engaging with an object, or that we begin analyzing our meditation, thinking, "It's going well now, this is correct." We must destroy these mental patterns because they are the opposite of meditation. If we don't destroy them, then it is like a person on a long journey who falls asleep on the road. He cannot reach the place.

Remain: After destroying the problems, meditate again in undistracted meditation. Stay on Natural Mind continuously without effort.

No. 24

All subject
and object are
included in
Natural Mind
without
separation.
All is
self-originated.

The Nature of Thoughts

Who here has not gone to the beach and marveled at the enormous storm surf breaking off-shore? It is awesome and beautiful. What a contrast to the sleepy lapping waves of calmer days! We see many waves, both those breaking at the shore and those that rise and fall in the deep ocean. There is a Buddhist analogy that makes use of this phenomena to illustrate the nature of thought. The ocean consists of vast, wide, and deep water; the waves, and especially the bigger waves, come up and look different from the rest of the ocean; but the waves, whether big or small, are the same water as the ocean and, you can say, are an expression of the nature of the ocean.

Thoughts that arise and fall away in our mind are the same nature as our Natural Mind and are an expression of it. They are not different and separate, just like the wave is only an expression of the sea.

No. 25

Grasping things as real
is the way you are deluded.
The absence of their self-nature
is the realization.

What is ego and ego-clinging?

Ego-clinging, both subtle and gross, is the root of samsara. It is the source of all suffering and negativity. The reason for this is that all misfortune and negativity comes from delusion. For example, attachment and anger arise from self-cherishing. Where does self-cherishing come from? It comes from ego-clinging.

Usually in our tradition, one of the important views is that the self does not exist. What is non-existent? Nothing exists that can be established from the object's own side. For example, when we go to church, we see the art or some statues on the wall. A guide points at the wall and says "this is Jesus" or "this is Mary". This is the view according to ordinary opinion. Actually it is only art. It is not true at all. It is not Jesus, nor Mary. We cannot find Jesus or Mary from the art's own side. Likewise for human beings, we have five aggregates—physical form, sensation, conception, formation, and consciousness. These are the bases for the designation of our conventional egos. But we cannot find that any of the five aggregates exist from their own side. This is what we call the non-existent self.

Otherwise we have a conventional view or nominal ego. For example, in reincarnation one can follow who came from the last life, is present in this life, and will be going to the next life. Another example is to follow someone who has not achieved full enlightenment, or will achieve full enlightenment. In these examples, we never separate from the nominal ego.

Ego-grasping is the opposite of self-cognizant wisdom. It is like being blind. Blind people would like to see a nice place and would like to enjoy a fuller life, but it is never that way. Like a blind person, we would like to realize everything with clarity, but we encounter a lot of obstacles due to self-cherishing and ego-clinging.

Our meditation works best for recognizing our ego or "I". However, sometimes we should look at the way things appear. For example, when you are thinking "I arise", the thought is very close and is connected to your ego. So you should think where does the "I" come from? What does "I" do? What are the conditions for "I"? How is ego the opposite condition to natural mind? This will help your meditation experience progress.

No. 26

The Natural Mind
is spontaneous.
It is not fabricated.
Because it is
not fabricated,
it is said that
it is without cause.

Beginning Experiences

We have been discussing a lot about the mind in meditation and now we have come to understand that meditation is all about getting an experience of the Natural Mind.

We've become aware of all the thoughts that draw our attention when we want to meditate. This is, in fact, our usual circumstance. We all have found ourselves deep in thought, only to "snap out of it" and notice we've been captured by an idea, a feeling or attachment to an object of our senses.

We engage in our thoughts, from one to the next, all day long. Our minds are like blades of grass bending any way the wind blows, depending on the next thought that comes. This is because we haven't really paid attention.

As we begin to meditate, we're aware of our thoughts coming and going. The advice is to let them arise and then fade without following them and without trying to stop them. This is the best way to attain meditation in Dzogchen. We can see our Natural Mind. We don't follow every thought like blades of grass in the wind.

No. 27

Natural Mind is
a result without a cause.
The perfect nature
is without effort
like the sky.
It is the supreme nature
over all results.

Signs of Success

We have learned to look for mind and to analyze "what is mind." The benefit of this is to get experience of the real condition of our mind. How does this help us?

As we observe how thoughts come and go, we can develop some control of our mind. We know that our actions and words and our every-day experiences are under the control of the mind and so, how beneficial would it be to be able to control the mind!

Then, as we progress, what signs might appear that indicate we have gained control over our mind? Here are some analogies for the meditator's steady, controlled mind:

- Like water going through a pipe, steady and with a continuous, stable flow

- Like a tortoise in a pan that never goes far from one spot

- Like a nail that is hammered in strongly.

No. 28

Impurities dissolve into
the Natural Mind.
Purity shines brightly.
Conception disappears
like taking off clothes.

Resting in the Natural Mind

According to Tantra, our bodies have wind energies in channels that support the mind's function. Like a rider who needs to know how to control the horse, breathing practices such as slowly inhaling and exhaling through the nostrils 21 times, may help calm and prepare the mind for meditation. As we calm the wind energy and then our mind, our body and speech automatically rest. All will spontaneously rest. The one with complete rest is the Enlightened One.

Sometimes we find that we are tired mentally and physically at the end of the day or at the end of the week. We can achieve a deep rest when we are able to rest in meditation on the Natural Mind. It is said that "we rest in the primordial panoramic awareness." Natural Mind is inconceivably vast, it is beginningless and is a pure awareness without thought of our past or future conditions. We rest in this pure expanse of mind.

No. 29

The great freedom
from limitation
is the best view.
This is also
the king of views.
It is very special
from others.
It is wonderful,
unlimited,
singular.

Contemplation

We contemplate our innate natural condition. As we have learned, we always follow our conceptions and thoughts. It has been like that for many lifetimes.

Consequently, we always have suffering and negativies arise. Then we feel sad about it. We feel sad and are also fearful that it will continue into the future.

How should we contemplate on the Natural Mind? The teaching says there are two connected aspects of contemplation: *Be in Freshness and Be Free from Effort*.

Don't doubt; you can be determined about this. You don't need to think about other things or look for any other meanings.

Freshness means to stay in the present without grasping at the present. If you stay in Freshness, you don't make any effort. You stay Natural, and then there is no Effort. This is how to contemplate for Natural Mind.

No. 30

If your meditation
stays on an object,
it is like floating there
and it is lost.
The traveler wants
to continue
and go far
but he falls asleep
by the road.

How Do We Contemplate?

Think—all appearances are combined with the space-like Natural Mind. We experience many thoughts coming while we are meditating. All are contained in the one space. When a thought comes, understand that it arises, abides and dissolves within the space-like Natural Mind. Conception, then, is not separate from the Natural Mind. It is like sugar dissolving into water; you can no longer distinguish it from the water. In the same way everything is unified within the Natural Mind.

The many phenomena—our appearances, good or bad feelings, thoughts and conceptions—are all in Natural Mind. They are not different or separate from it.

Remain in the state—we now stay in the state of Natural Mind. We have dissolved conception into the Natural Mind and now we remain without doing anything more or changing anything. We remain in the space-like quality.

No. 31

If your practice
follows the correct way
and is strong,
the three steps
gradually appear
according to
different levels
of capacity.

Three Steps to Realization in Dzogchen Practice

According to Dzogchen, it is most important to realize the view in practice. Realization means how much you view appearance as self-originated wisdom, meaning there is no other source besides the self for appearances. Step by step through your meditation, more and more can appear without your becoming distracted. Three main levels, each with three subcategories, are explained in Dzogchen teachings: session meditation *(Thun Gom)*, habitual meditation *(Ngang Gom)*, and supreme meditation *(Long Gom)*.

1) For beginner practitioners, distractions, agitations and many obstacles arise most of the time and may appear as feelings of doubt, fear, and sadness. Then at times, self-originated wisdom

can appear like sun light with many clouds in the sky. The most important thing to do when you have a problem is to try again and again, making the effort to meditate continuously. If you can progress in this way, one day originated wisdom can appear and it will be more pleasing to meditate.

2) The second step is becoming aware that the view of appearances in the first step is a mind-made fabrication. The important thing here is to continue to meditate—effortlessly. When you progress, all conceptions become a friend and multiplicity appears as one taste. It is also important to train by using a variety of positive and negative objects in your practice. The application of mindfulness should be used to retain awareness on the natural state and seal all phenomena within originated wisdom in your realization.

3) When you get to the third step of supreme meditation, in practice, you have totally exhausted any effort to maintain subject and object. Your meditation is stable and you remain day and night on non-meditation and without distraction. At this level, you can automatically cut through thought and ordinary awareness, because they are not necessary to your practice. Finally, you achieve the great non-meditation level; only names or labels are left for all phenomenal appearances. All phenomena are exhausted and unchanging in the natural state. When you reach this level of practice, you have fully achieved supreme realization. This is what we call attaining the state of Buddhahood.

No. 32

Nature, Circumstance and Mistaking
are the three faults of laxity
Laxity diminishes the purity
of the meditation.

Solving Laxity

There can be many faults that occur during our meditation. The two main ones are laxity and agitation and there are gross and subtle forms of these.

In this lesson, we address laxity, or dullness in meditation. There are three main causes of laxity: Nature, Circumstance and Mistaking.

Nature—We can experience laxity if one of our 4 elements is out of balance. For example, if the earth element is dominant then it's easy to experience laxity. Nature can also relate to the basic level of intelligence of the meditator.

Circumstance—We can have laxity with hard physical work, clothes that are too warm, hot weather or overeating.

Mistaking—A person may make a mistake and not care about it, for example trying to stay awake. They don't think it's a problem.

Solutions: Assume the correct meditative posture, elevate the mind by remembering the benefits and good results of meditation, remember the qualities of Dharmakaya, clean your environment, take a break, change your seat, go to a high place, eat less, sing or chant, and lift your eyes or gaze at the sky.

No. 33

Agitation
is the mind
going everywhere.
Like the cloud
that goes wherever
the wind blows.

Solving Agitation

The two main faults in meditation are laxity and agitation. In this lesson we address agitation or excessive thinking. There are three main causes of agitation: Nature, Circumstance and Mistaking.

Nature: The 4 elements are not balanced. If the fire or wind element is dominant then it's easy to experience agitation. An imbalance of the elements can also lead to anger or pride which can contribute to agitation.

Circumstance: Some people have a propensity to follow ordinary perceptions which can interfere with meditation. For example, if one watches a lot of TV, even if the programs have no meaning, or they like to talk a lot with people, the mind is distracted.

Mistaking: They think there's no need to meditate. They say there is no benefit to meditation. Their mind goes a lot and they can't control it.

Solutions:
- Assume the correct body posture
- Sit on a smooth and warm cushion
- Massage with medicine and oil
- Relax the body and mind.

In everything you do, go slowly—like walking, talking or daily tasks. Eat heavier nutritious foods. Meditation will also solve agitation with practice.

No. 34

Whatever you see, it is.
Look directly.
If you don't see,
did you look?
You have seen
Natural Mind.

Self-Liberation in the Natural Mind View

"A curled up snake will naturally unwind when the snake starts to move away—just by itself." Now, when we recognize Natural Mind, ignorance disappears by itself. This is self-liberation.

For example, when we're angry, understand that the source of the anger is the Natural Mind and is not separate from it. When you find the source of anger in Natural Mind, then the anger disappears by itself. It is self-liberated.

Everything is the same condition. Big subjects like ignorance are the cause of suffering, nirvana and samsara, as well as small subjects like delusion, conception, and anger—all dissolves into Natural Mind. We want to be liberated from suffering. Everything comes from and disappears into Natural Mind; therefore Natural Mind is Self-Liberation Wisdom.

No. 35

Self-originated wisdom
is the foundation.
The five delusions
are manifestations.

Self-Knowing Wisdom

"The light of the lamp is self clear." It is said that the light is "self clear" because it is not obscured to itself. It is possible for other conditions to obscure it, but to itself, it remains always unobscured. Why do we say Natural Mind is self-knowing? Natural Mind is also not hidden to itself. We have heard that it is beyond mind and beyond speech. When we recognize it, then we see it clearly, but it is always apparent to itself. So, we say it is Self-Knowing.

Then why is it wisdom? While there are many conceptions and delusions which obscure the Natural Mind, our ignorance is the main obscuration which prevents our seeing it. This ignorance is the source of our suffering, and recognizing the Natural Mind is the antidote to that ignorance. It is the ultimate truth. This is the best wisdom.

No. 36

Ultimate truth is like space,
beyond phenomena
that originates or ceases.
It is beyond sentences,
unthinkable and
inexpressible with words.

Dispense with Words, Engage with Meaning

Normally we pay attention while we are listening to teachings, reading books or studying. We rely on words and group them into sentences. This is very important for us in the beginning.Later, we dispense with words and rely on their meaning.

Ultimate truth can't be experienced with mind, because mind is conventional. So all words, speech and sentences follow mind and its motivation. Listening to sentences is only the first step. When we reach the second step, meaning beyond convention, we don't depend on words anymore.

Why did the Buddha give so many teachings? It is because people didn't understand ultimate truth. When they under-stand, what use are words? For example, when we've finished crossing the water and we've reached our destination, we no longer need the boat.

Buddha taught many methods to understand ultimate truth but all were to explain one single point. Every teaching was meant to lead to ultimate truth. The words are not important, the meaning is important. This meaning is the Natural Mind.

No. 37

If the five consciousnesses
follow the five objects,
don't cling to ego.
If you cling to ego,
don't be habitual.

Proceed Along the Path

Ordinary thoughts proceed along the path in Natural Mind meditation. The teachings say that in one day, we humans have 84,000 thoughts arising, including delusions and mental troubles. Natural Mind meditation is the one way to proceed along the path. What is this way? Whatever conception arises, we don't make any effort to abandon it. Also we don't engage with the concepts that arise. There are three levels for proceeding on the path.

For the highest and best level, when concepts come, the practitioner recognizes that they are definitely manifestations of Natural Mind and they dissolve into Natural Mind like snowflakes falling on the ocean.

For the second highest level, when thoughts arise, it is like sunlight melting the frost on the leaves in the autumn morning. This practitioner uses meditation as an antidote to concepts. They depend on meditation to solve the problem.

For the third level, the practitioner uses mindfulness. For example, a very angry person accepts the advice of someone and so they become calm. They recognize the unwanted results of anger such as fighting, bad relations in the future and upset for everyone. They practice patience instead of being angry, because they recognize that this brings peacefulness and future good relations. This is mindfulness.

These three levels depend on the person's realization of Natural Mind.

No. 38

If I understand everything —
All conduct is enlightened
being's conduct.
It is boundless,
immeasurable.

Utilizing the Varieties of Conduct

We have learned about three levels of practitioners: Low, Medium, and High Levels of Realization. A person will have different experiences dependant upon their level of realization.

There are three modes of conduct for each of these three levels:

Low Realization: Like a candle, the flame is easily disturbed by the wind. Beginning practitioners, using conduct of body and speech, try to control obstacles and work to facilitate positive conditions for practice. For example, they practice the Six Perfections.

Medium Realization: The conduct of body, speech and ordinary actions become a friend to practice. For example, we refrain from seeing something as good or bad, clean or dirty, or enemies and friends; we refrain from placing a value on the object. If there is a big fire, the wind serves to help the fire become larger. Like a baby, we do not stop or criticize thoughts. We become free free from suppressing or cultivating thoughts.

Higher Realization: The conduct here is called "Multiplicity as Being One Taste" or "Victory Over Prejudice." For example, when we get to a golden place, everything there is gold. The practitioner understands that all is a manifestation of Natural Mind and not separate.

Each style of conduct is dependent upon one's level of realization.

No. 39

Undistracted
and Non-meditation
is meditation.
The Natural Mind
is non-meditation.
Like a nail
pounded into wood,
meditation needs to
be undistracted.

Undistracted Non-meditation

There are two important qualities of uncontrived meditation: undistracted and non-meditation.

Non-meditation: Natural Mind meditation is uncontrived. It is and must be without effort because when we make an effort we are changing something. Then that is not meditation. The teaching says, "be uncontrived in single-pointed contemplation." This is non-meditation. It is said, "without-effort, meditation is non-meditation."

Undistracted: What is undistracted? For example, in the mirror, there may appear many different forms and colors. They appear but do not disturb the glass. Like this, when you contemplate in uncontrived meditation, phenomena such as thoughts and conceptions appear but they don't disturb the meditation.

Undistracted means continuously staying on Natural Mind. When we meditate we stay in the uncontrived condition and we don't lose the meditative balance.

No. 40

When practitioners
have a deep
understanding of
beyond partiality,
they become
confident of the
Dzogchen view.

Non-Partiality: View According to Dzogchen

The Great Perfection is the view free from limitations. It is unconfined and unrestricted and without partiality.

When we attain higher realization, the meditation is not separate from experience; it is also the Dzogchen view. We understand that phenomena arise and they don't make us happy or unhappy. When something good happens normally we get happy and we get sad when something bad happens. With higher realization, we don't get affected like this.

With higher realization, the conduct of body, speech and mind are in a uncontrived state. View, meditation, and conduct are the same value. Everything is made into the same taste.

Many Dzogchen masters studied sutra, tantra and many practices. They can bring all practices into their Dzogchen practice as the same taste. They become confident in the Dzogchen view and so can practice different lineages without any of them harming the other. It only benefits.

The foundation of Dzogchen is inclusive, with no partiality. Many Rimé masters practice in a non-sectarian way and do practices from many lineages and schools. *Ris* in Tibetan means one-sided or partisan and *med* means not. Together it is Rimé.

No. 41

The three phenomena
are exhausted in
intrinsic awareness.
All of Samsara
and Nirvana are
exhausted in the
Primordial State.

Knowing One Liberates All

How do we clear misconceptions according to the Dzogchen tradition? There are two kinds of phenomena, subtle and gross, and both manifest from the ground of Natural Mind. At the most subtle level, sounds, colors and lights appear. For the highest practitioner, these most subtle appearances are recognized as a manifestation of Natural Mind. For example, the practitioner may recognize three phenomena as appearing in the bardo or intermediate state at the time of rebirth. They occur at a very subtle level. The ground of Natural Mind and its manifestations are connected in a special way. The three appearances of sounds, colors, and lights, are manifestations of the ground of Natural Mind. Whoever knows this condition will find it easy to become liberated.

In another example, as grosser phenomena such as ignorance, anger and strong emotions arise, we should recognize that they have the same connection with the foundation of Natural Mind.

We should recognize both subtle and gross appearances as manifestations of the ground of Natural Mind. This is called "Knowing One Liberates All."

No. 42

There is no
foundation in any object.
Whatever you think,
it appears
that way to you.
It is like the six ways
that water appears
to beings of the six realms.

Five Pointing Out Instructions

There are Five Steps of pointing-out instructions that lead to deeper and deeper recognition of Natural Mind.

1. There is no source other than our mind for the six sense phenomena. Recognize that phenomena are only mind.

2. Whatever appears is connected and selfless. Recognize that the mind is empty.

3. The meditation experience appears in the nature of one's self-luminous mind. Recognize that emptiness is luminosity.

4. Whatever phenomena appear, it is positive and helpful, like a friend. Recognize luminosity is in union with emptiness.

5. Whatever experience appears, it is undistracting. It is like brandishing a spear in space and all obscurations disappear. Finally, everything is clear like a crystal sphere. All outer and inner appearances are clear. Recognize that union as great bliss.

No. 43

The Nature of Mind
is primordially pure
and unborn
because there is neither
a subject
nor an object
of grasping.

Commitment in Dzogchen

Many teachings have been given about commitment, or samaya. These commitments are in all of the vehicles of Buddhism (for example, respect to dharma texts, holy teachings, and lineages). Four commitments are taught that are exclusive to Dzogchen: non-existence, all-pervasiveness, oneness, and spontaneous presence.

1. Non-existence: The Nature of Mind is primordially pure. When we abide in the Natural State, there is no grasper of existence, nor object of grasping. There is neither stopping nor creating. There is no "I" or "me" (subject or object).

2. All-Pervasiveness: The Natural State is free from observance of vows. There is neither beginning nor end. There is no foundation of fixed time.

3. Oneness: All phenomena are unified into oneness. The Natural State has no "I" or "me," only oneness. Within oneness, the three times cannot be explained.

4. Spontaneous Presence: The Natural State does not need to be sought; it is spontaneously present, with primordially spontaneous enlightened quality.

No. 44

Confusion dissolves
into the natural state
like clouds into sky,
revealing purity
and luminosity.
Removing the clothing
of conceptual thought,
naked awareness
is revealed.

Discerning Mind and Awareness

All consciousness and mental factors are conventional truth. This includes what arises in mind, specific details of experience. In some Buddhist schools, there are references to the consciousnesses. In Tibetan psychology, there are many mental factors. All of these are mind, including thoughts, conceptions, and delusions, as well as positive objects, like compassion and love. The ground and path of Sutra and Tantra are part of the conventional mind, as are mantra, yoga, and visualization of deities.

According to Dzogchen, these are all mind grasping onto positive and negative objects and thoughts. Therefore, they are not perfected, in that, as mind, the conventional thoughts are polluted with ignorance and delusion.

Awareness is objectless and without grasping of inert nature, effortless, and beyond conceptual mind—the self-knowing state of awakened mind. We discern the difference between awareness and the conceptual mind through meditation. When we meditate, our mind is calm and in the natural state. Dirty water, when left alone, settles and becomes clear. Similarly, when we meditate, thoughts dissipate. Staying on awareness, thoughts disappear. What is important is not whether the meditation is good or bad, but what is conventional truth and what is awareness.

No. 45

Self-originated
wisdom is freely
all-pervasive.
Ignorance is
fully self-conquered.

Self-Originated Wisdom

The natural mind is self-originated wisdom, with many special qualities, one of which is that it is self-originated. "Self-originated" means unborn and unobstructed. It is unborn because it has no primary or secondary causes. The primary cause is the main cause, which is transformed into the effect, like a seed transforms into a fruit. The secondary cause is temporary, a supporter of fruition, like water, sun, and soil, that supports a seed's growth. All conventional realities come from these two causes.

The nature of mind is primordially Buddhahood. It cannot be liberated or obstructed by anything—antidote or object.

The essence of the natural state is primordially without dependence on other, and is primordially self-knowing. Therefore, it is called self-originated wisdom or, in Tibetan, Rangbyung Yeshi. It's imagined like this: the sun shines, and the darkness is gone automatically. There is never ignorance in the foundation of the natural mind. A person who knows this condition has recognized self-originated wisdom.

No. 46

A bird without wings
has no method to fly.

Take courage, energize,
practice, and look to
the natural state.

Appearance of Inner Wisdom

Some important conditions are necessary for meditation and practice: good weather, appropriate food and drink, and the proper time and place. These are always important for beginning practitioners.

For a very fortunate person, the wisdom directly appears when the teacher introduces it for the first time. Most people need to go step-by-step. The following are examples of three levels of practice.

Example of the first level: There are many clouds in the sky. We cannot always see the sun. We can only see the sun occasionally. Likewise, there are many obstacles to seeing wisdom. Beginning practitioners may need to develop stability in practice, and not be discouraged when clouds of doubt arise in their minds.

Example of the second level: The sunlight pervades the sky, shining in all directions. With experience, the doubts of practitioners are cleared away. They get confidence of the view of wisdom and meditation.

Example of the third level: In a golden land, everything appears golden. For practitioners, what arises is always wisdom. What they do in body, speech, and mind cannot depart from wisdom. The teachings say there are many manifestations of wisdom: 84 thousand wisdoms, 61 wisdoms, and 5 wisdoms. One who meditates sees all of the wisdoms.

No. 47

Waves disappear
into the ocean,
planets disappear
into space,
and phenomena
disappears into
the nature of mind.

Cutting Through or Trek Chöd

In Tibetan, "Trek Chöd" is defined as "cutting through" doubt and delusion to primordial Buddhahood. Some teachings say that Trek Chöd is a lazy person's practice to quickly realize enlightenment without effort.

Primordial Buddhahood has four modes of liberation. A practitioner completely recognizes oneself, absolutely remains without doubt, continues directly with confidence in liberation, and continuously practices the primordial natural state as described. For this reason, this is called, "cutting through practice."

In Trek Chöd practice, there is neither ground nor path as described in other vehicles. Multiple antidotes are not needed for multiple negativities; there is just one antidote for samsara. There is neither ceasing nor creating of thoughts in the natural state. Phenomena and all negative thoughts are directly liberated into the innate natural state of their origination. There is no negativity, samsara, or suffering.

Anything whatsoever that appears, all phenomena, become a friend of your practice. As an example, when robbers come into a house and look around to take something, they return with empty hands because the house is empty. Through this practice, step-by-step, the root of grasping thoughts is reduced, liberating the karmic obscurations into intrinsic awareness. For this reason, it is called cutting through.

No. 48

Phenomena do not just
finish or stop. They trace back
to the origin and are finally
liberated.

"Thod Gel" Direct Crossing

Thod Gel comes only after "Trek Chöd" practice has already been well established. Then, the practitioner can make a lot of effort to visualize luminosities. For example, the light of a candle in a vase comes up and over the glass. Our awareness is located in our heart, and the channels form a path, and the eyes are like a door. "Thod Gel" practice tries to make wisdom apparent through the eyes.

There are four key points in Thod Gel practice. The first key point is like a watchman at the door. It is actually seeing by personal observation. The second key point is illustrated by the example of a guesthouse, where the object is stable and non-changing. The objects of sky, sun, moon, and lamplight remain when we see them through our eyes. The third key point defines the wind and breath, which should be careful and slow like robbers walking into a house. The exhalation and inhalation come out very slowly through the teeth. The fourth key point of awareness is like bright sunlight, which makes luminosities apparent. During this time, keep your mind resting on unconditional dharmakaya, objectless and without grasping. With this practice, luminosities can appear, regardless of brightness and dimness.

Practitioners get many indications of experience through this practice, such as space as a dome of light or wisdom appearing as spheres. Also, an indicator of wisdom is Buddha's body as uninterrupted spheres and light. The teachings say that for practitioners who make great effort for liberation in this practice, it does not depend on their created karma, dullness or sharpness. The "Thod Gel" practice has four steps for the appearance of luminosities. Finally, all luminosities are exhausted and dissolve into the foundation of primordially pure outer phenomena. Also dissolved are the outer phenomena, the inner body, in between moments of wind and thoughts, resulting in the accomplishment of the great rainbow body.

No. 49

Dualistic thought
is subject and object.
Nihilism is the absence of
the appearance
of phenomena.
The Middle Way
is free from extremes.
The correct realization
is beyond the
four extremes.

The View of Non-Dual Grasper and Grasping

What is grasper and grasping? It is object and subject. When an object first appears in the mind of a sentient being, attachment arises and generates a stream of thoughts. For example, insects become bound to a spider's web; the more the insect's body moves, the more it becomes bound in the web. All ignorance and the idea of "You" and "I" comes from grasper and grasping. Ego-grasping is part of that. The cause of samsara ultimately arises in this way.

Karma comes from delusion and delusion comes from an ego-grasping view. For example, on a dark night when we see something long and thin which is actually a multi-colored rope, we might think that it looks like a snake. We look at it and think it is a real snake; we become afraid. This fear is created out of grasping onto a mistaken perception. However, when the object appears to the practitioner, it is immediately integrated into the Natural State; it is dissolved into Ultimate Truth. There is no foundation of attachment. At that time the practitioner observes without a grasping view. For example, when we meditate in the Natural State, there is no object and subject.

Why is the grasping view a mistaken perception? Whatever first appears—where did it originate? Where is it abiding? To where will it disappear? Everything is pervaded with intrinsic awareness. It is non-dual within the natural state. According to high practitioners, there is no rejection, no negativity. If you visualize a golden place, you will not find earth and stone there. When we meditate we must continue our session without grasping. There is no difference between the observer and the observed. It is non-duality. This is what we call "self-knowing wisdom." When we experience this, we overcome straying and confusion. Automatically, we get liberated or achieve Enlightenment.

No. 50

If given a name,
someone becomes
attached to it.
If this becomes
attachment,
one becomes bound.
If one becomes bound,
it is deviation
from one's practice.
If it is deviation
from one's practice,
one wanders
in cyclic existence.

Non-Action and Without a Trace

From the Dzogchen perspective, we have view, meditation and conduct. We call these three things non-action (without effort) and without a trace. This should be without effort for any actions, beyond grasping at thoughts and beyond words and speech. The Natural Mind has no cause. It cannot be counted. From this perspective, there is no need for hope and fear. The Natural Mind is never created by Buddhas or gods and cannot be changed by an intelligent person. This is why we can call this non-action.

What is "without a trace"? An example would be when a bird flies in the sky—there is no trace. The meaning for Dzogchen meditation and view is that there is no beginning or origin. There is no place of abiding at the present time. Also, in the future, there is no place where one goes. The view is without watching. The meditation is without meditating. The conduct is without activities. The conceptions, delusions and negativities actually have no foundation. In our practice, when these arise, we can observe them. They will be liberated into the Natural State. This is "without a trace." In summary, we call this practice "non-action and without a trace."

No. 51

As the Mind
is focused
on the object,
discursive thoughts
are calmed
more and more,
and wisdom arises
more and more.

Calm abiding and Insight Meditation in Dzogchen

According to Dzogchen, there are three meditation methods:
- shamatha or calm abiding
- vipashyana, insight, and the
- union of shamatha and vipashyana.

We can explain that there are two kinds of shamatha methods, general and specific. The general method for very beginning practitioners is to gaze at an object, such as a small statue or Tibetan Ah syllable with concentration. Later, as one progresses, the mind becomes more calm and comfortable and can stay focused on the object for longer times. In all, there are nine steps in the practice of general shamatha.

In Dzogchen, even if you haven't achieved the top level of experience for general shamatha, it is necessary to practice fixing and calming the mind. Specific to Dzogchen shamatha, the aspect of focus is the emptiness quality of originated wisdom. When originated wisdom is realized, all phenomena are origin (primordial)—arising, abiding and disappearing in the primordial ocean—this is the reason why it is called calm abiding.

In Dzogchen, vipashyana has the luminous quality of inner wisdom. Self-knowing reveals the luminous quality of self-knowing wisdom. Visions and sounds can be clear and naked as luminosities appear through a variety of experience. What are the signs of the inner luminosity? An example of appearance luminosity is someone in dark retreat who attains the ability to read, write and see forms without normal light. We can recognize inner luminosity through the method of meditation on the Natural Mind. Shamatha and vipashyana are unified in the natural state. How do you get this type of realization and experience? If we have shamatha, the emptiness quality inherently has luminosity qualities which arise spontaneously in your experience and realization. When we meditate on the Natural Mind, shamatha and vipashyana are included in the practice—in union.

No. 52

In Dzogchen,
students who
are worthy vessels
pursue extreme conduct
without distinguishing
such conduct as
better or worse.

Three Activities Along the Dzogchen Path

The activities of body, speech and mind can help carry us along the Dzogchen path.

As a beginner, we strive to attain a stable, undistracted, non-meditative state. As we progress, we include or mix in activities little by little, developing experience, checking success by measuring our undisturbed natural state. Eventually, all activities become a friend to practice.

In a beginning body practice, we start with a basic sitting posture. As we progress, we can include eye or arm or leg movement;

then we check our meditative state. If we are able to maintain our stability, we can proceed by standing, walking, circumambulating, prostrating, etc. Eventually, we can include even more vigorous activities such as jumping and running—that is, we can include all physical activities. Maintaining a meditative state during these movements generates success for carrying us along the Dzogchen path through the body.

In basic speech practice, we are quiet. With more experience, we can incorporate mantra and prayers. Checking each step of the way, we can proceed to maintaining a meditative state undisturbed while speaking with people, singing. or laughing. We can even enter into debate. Maintaining a meditative state is a measure of success along the Dzogchen path through speech.

In basic mind practice with meditation, we still the mind and rest in the natural state. For example, with more experience, we can engage in positive activities such as visualizing oneself as a deity or a Buddha. If you are without disturbance of mind, you can increase the visualization to include more aspects including all enlightened qualities, the mandala and so on. With success, further activities include analyzing any arising phenomena, thoughts and emotions. These activities are used to measure success along the Dzogchen path through mind.

The activities of body, speech and mind are used to bring success and much benefit through freedom from attachment, suffering, fear, hope, obstacles, difficulties and death.

No. 53

Be attentive
to how your mind
grasps discursive thoughts.
If you stay on great bliss,
it will return and
pacify by itself.

Remedies for Meditating with Arising Conceptions

When we meditate, many thoughts arise as distractions. What can we do to overcome this? We can incorporate these three methods into our practice.

Example 1: A robber sees a house without people and enters to take something. He doesn't find anything inside the house. On another day, when he sees the house again, he already knows that it is empty.

The meaning: In the beginning, we look for the source of thoughts, which is empty. Upon achieving realization (liberation into the natural state), if thoughts arise, one immediately recognizes the natural condition.

Example 2: A person in a boat has a bird. The bird flies away from the boat. It returns later without the person waiting for it.

The meaning: When we meditate, thoughts travel around, but we do not necessarily wait for them to return. Thoughts will return and when they do, we recognize their condition. There is no separation in the natural state.

Example 3: Clouds move in the space of sky. There is no other source without space.

The meaning: The truth is that thoughts arise, abide, and disappear in the natural state. This is what we call self-clearing practice or self-purifying practice.

No. 54

In a summer marsh,
plants grow as
whatever they may.
In sage realization,
appearances of
exceptional experiences
appear as whatever they may.

Exceptional Experiences and Realization

Exceptional experiences are something uncertain with a great variety of feelings and thoughts. The three major categories of exceptional experiences are called bliss experiences, clarity experiences and non-thought experiences. These experiences arise through all meditations—shamatha, vipassana, mahamudra, and of course, in Dzogchen meditation. These experiences of meditation can occur across religious traditions.

1) During meditation, bliss experiences can arise equally through your body and mind. The feeling is very smooth, joyful, blissful, and with great happiness. When your mind is relaxed, completely at ease, and you feel unobstructed in your practice, realization of the union of emptiness and clarity appear.

2) Clarity experiences display a feeling of wakefulness, including appearances like moonlight, daybreak, or sitting in a very bright tent. Sometimes your body feels very light, like feathers. You can feel joy and happiness. With clarity, one can continuously maintain a very stable meditation without conception.

3) The non-thought experiences may occur during meditation when you do not lose stability on the natural state. Concepts do not arise and one does not follow thought. You feel an experience of realization of your natural mind; it is beyond words like a mute dream. There is no illustration of any objects.

The teaching says if you attain some of these experiences, you still cannot be satisfied with your practice and you must continue to progress. Realization means the intrinsic awareness of Primordial Buddhahood is realized step by step in practice. There are many levels for development for realization.

However, in Dzogchen, exceptional experiences are always clearly distinguished from realization.

No. 55

The luminosity
is an essence
and the emptiness
is the nature of
Dharmakaya.
When realized,
all Buddhas' activities
for sentient beings
automatically arise.

Essence, Nature and Compassion

In Dzogchen teachings, the natural state has three important qualities: essence (Ngobo), nature (Rang zhin), and compassion (Thug Je). The reason and motivation to develop this practice is to achieve buddhahood and engage in activities for the benefit of all sentient beings.

According to the Dzogchen view, there is a basic foundation— the fundamental great primordial purity. It appears after you have recognized the nature of mind. You feel something as if you are looking at the ocean. There are many waves coming and going every moment, but they are not separate from the ocean and the ocean is the basic ground of all of them. This is the emptiness quality of the natural mind. We call it the essence of the natural state.

The second quality is what we call nature luminosity or clarity. It is like a candle placed into a vase. It remains vividly clear in the moment and is the source of the surrounding light. That is great luminosity. It is the source and manifestation of the power of the three great phenomena—sound, color, and light. There are always enlightenment bodies and wisdoms spontaneously included in the luminosity quality. For example, during the intermediate state after death, we experience the appearance of five different lights and five different realms.

Compassion is the third quality of the natural state; it is the unity of emptiness and clarity and is unobstructed from any appearance in the natural state. From the unity of essence emptiness and natural luminosity, one undertakes activities for the benefit of all sentient beings. In the great unity quality of compassion, one devotes activities through emanating for all sentient beings.

When a practitioner attains higher realization, when the five lights arise during the intermediate state, one is able to maintain the natural condition. At that time, practitioners can realize the illusion of body, speech, mind, object, or whatever appears. Five different lights, five different pure lands, five different deities and mandalas can all appear. When we understand the natural state, there can be many activities for the benefit of all sentient beings through the quality of compassion.

No. 56

Phenomena
do not just
finish or stop.
They trace
back to the
origin and
finally return to
the source and
are liberated.

The Inseparable Two Truths in Dzogchen

Buddha taught 84,000 methods including 360 categories of teachings for understanding the nature of mind. Fundamental to these teachings are the two truths: relative and ultimate. The cause of most sentient beings' ignorance and delusion is tied to the misconceptions of their minds, so it is very difficult to understand the inseparable two truths. It is hidden within realization.

Ordinary people believe whatever they see or think and they build onto that view with additional thoughts and grasping. According to ordinary view, it appears true for them. But it is actually not true; it is like illusion. If a magician displays illusions to audiences, like elephants and horses, some audience members may think they real. Like that, for ordinary people, appearances exist as objects—good, bad, friend, enemy, beautiful, ugly, positive, negative, etc. Why is it called relative truth? It means ordinary appearances are actually false.

The other truth is called ultimate truth. When an illusion is displayed, the magician already knows that the illusion is not true. Like that, one realizes that all phenomenal appearances are pervaded by ultimate truth. For those who attain the higher experience of the Dzogchen view, they see that phenomena are manifested by the nature of mind. They realize that there is no truly existent positive or negative qualities within the objects. It is realized that all phenomena are sealed into one single sphere of ultimate truth. No one can be separated from the ultimate truth.

The teachings say that these views are the inseparable two truths. One can clear away the extremes of eternalism and nihilism through this point of view. Particular to Dzogchen, there is only one truth because the single sphere view.

No. 57

Some fortunate ones
who possess
profound certainty,
break the three seals
and then complete the three
dynamic energies.

Manifesting the Ground-appearance

The basic ground is never defiled. It is undisturbed by phenomena. As an example, clouds arise and dissolve within the sky with no effect upon the sky. There are two kinds of ground-appearance: pure and impure.

For the experienced practitioner, at the very beginning, a co-emergent wisdom appears simultaneously with the subtle three phenomena. Those who already realize and experience whatever appears to them as object, forms, sounds, and colors are not truly existent and are like illusion, who remain continuously in a primordially enlightened state, can emanate many different Buddhas' body, speech, and mind for the benefit of sentient beings.

For ordinary people, when beginning appearances of the subtle three phenomena simultaneous arise, the subtle mind analyzes the phenomenal subtle forms, sounds, and colors; this is called co-emergent ignorance. Why ignorance? An example is when we look in a mirror and it reflects our face; what is perceived is not a real face. Like that, the ignorance confuses and identifies the object as opposite of the true condition.

Instantly after that, the gross mind arises and grasps the object; this is called conceptual ignorance. This ignorance comes from the co-emergent ignorance and strengthens the mind's grasping or holding on to extreme beliefs and states of mistaken perception.

Those who have not understood and are without realization about the true condition of the ground-appearance will always have trouble, even at the important time of the intermediate state. At that time, primordial Buddhahood will appear, but it will not be recognized.

Without experience, the result is to circle in the three realms and six classes of beings and there will be a lot of suffering in the future life. So realization depends upon the experience of the ground-appearance of the true condition.

No. 58

The other vehicles' faults
are pacified without rejection.
The other vehicles' good qualities
are effortlessly and spontaneously
included in Dzogchen.

Ultimate nature is revealed only through Dzogchen

In the Tibetan tradition, the teachings are generally given according to two different systems: nine vehicles or three vehicles. In either system, Dzogchen is the completion vehicle.

In an example, some blind people surround and touch an elephant in order to describe it. One person describes the elephant as tall; one person touches its tail and says the elephant is like a snake; one person touches its ears and describes the elephant as looking like leaves; and one person feels a tusk and says the elephant looks like a horn. Each describes a part of the elephant's body, but none find the correct or entire view of the elephant.

In either vehicle system, the lower vehicles are like this—only a part of the true condition is understood. But in ninth or final vehicle of Dzogchen, the complete view is revealed, encompassing all the qualities of the lower vehicles.

No. 59

Sound manifests as
self-originated sound,
light is like sunlight
or a rainbow,
and rays are like
a net of sunbeams.
These are the qualities of the
primordial natural state.

Forceful Method for Recognizing Luminosity

Your natural state has two qualities: emptiness and luminosity. There is no need to explain more than these qualities. Emptiness is basic space. Luminosity has three appearance qualities: color, sound, and rays. The source exists only within; there is nothing that exists from outside.

The important quality we must recognize and believe in is the luminosity from inner wisdom. For that, there is a very important and forceful method for the recognition the luminosity from inside.

Sit comfortably on the cushion or chair and breathe in. Block your ears with your thumbs, block your nostrils with your little fingers, and block your eyes your other fingers. Hold your breath a moment and relax in the natural state. Three luminosities can appear simultaneously. When you have these luminosities appear, remember that they are just manifestations of the basic space. It is like sun and sunlight or ocean and waves. The teaching says that when you have experience with this practice, you can develop it. Therefore, you can recognize the quality of luminosity, even during the intermediate state after death.

No. 60

This is the essence
of ultimate teaching:
when someone is
afraid of it,
they have been
confused in the
small mind of the
lower vehicle.

The Defilement of Doubt

There are many obstacles to the complete fulfillment of one's practice. One serious problem is doubt. It is a pitfall that can be a very big obstacle to recognizing the Natural Mind in the Dzogchen path. How does it harm our practice? Normally, we see doubt arise from causes such as these:

1) We think we are ordinary sentient beings, that we don't have the enlightened quality, and that we will always have a difficult life.

2) During meditation, when abiding in the natural state without focusing on a particular object or visualization, we do not feel satisfied.

3) We think we can engage in positive activities through using our ordinary mind, even though the teaching says the ultimate truth is inconceivable.

4) We deny that there is no separation of cause and effect; liberation cannot occur from God or a Buddha, but only through our own primordially pure quality.

5) We fail to practice direct fulfillment of primordial purity awareness, as all methods integrate into the single practice.

The teaching says that one's thoughts are too habituated with perceptions of self, which prevents us from recognizing Natural Mind. So the teaching introduces you to the qualities of Natural Mind, but doubt can be a powerful obstacle to achieving it.

No. 61

You see
appearances
as your own face.
Like seeing
your face reflected
in a mirror.

Phenomena is an Extremely Good Teacher

Whatever we see or think, we form a strong grasping onto the object. Then those objects immediately change and disappear because they do not have an independent foundation. All objects depend on other objects. They look like they are independent when we don't check their origin. When we truly investigate the origin of phenomena, it is not stable.

For example, some practitioners live under the tree; the tree's leaves grow, fall, and change with the seasons. Some practitioners live in a house without a roof; they can see the stars move around in the sky at night. Some practitioners live near a cemetery; they can see dead bodies - new, young, old, rotten, dry, or divided into parts. These are examples of finding the natural mind through the changing of phenomena.

Look at a car; it is compounded by many parts. If you separate those different parts from each other, you cannot find where the car is. It is the same with human beings. We appear as an independent "I," but as we investigate ourselves, when we observe our true condition, we never find the "I" or the "you."

Phenomena is always showing the true condition of an object, but the ordinary mind does not recognize it. Practitioners, however, have a better chance for realizing true nature. One means of discovering where appearances come from is by finding where they dissolve. If we realize this meaning, then phenomena has taught us the ultimate truth. So when we have higher experiences, all appearances become a friend to our practice. According to accomplished practitioners, phenomena have already become their extremely good teacher.

Acknowledgments

Gratitude for all those who reviewed, edited and contributed their efforts in the production of this book. In particular, I would like to express heartfelt gratitude to all of my dharma students, especially Elizabeth Hannah, Antoinette Bauer-Smedberg, Lara Summerville, Nancy Kvam, Kate Hitt, Michael Roth, Mark Sorensen, and Donald Davies.

I would also like to express my appreciation to the Kunsang Gar Board members and sangha for their continuing support and participation in many great Dharma activities, out of which this book has come to fruition.

About the Author

Geshe Dangsong Namgyal is a teacher, author, poet, and meditation master. Born in Tibet, he entered the monastery at a young age, beginning his study of the foundations of Buddhism and Bon Dzogchen. In 1991, he left Tibet in order to receive more advanced teachings in Nepal and India. For many years, he studied logic, Buddhist psychology, Prajnaparamita and Madhyamika in the Nalanda tradition at Sera Je Monastery. In the Bon Monasteries of Menri and Triten Norbutse, he concentrated his studies on sutra, tantra and Dzogchen. After 25 years of study and meditation, he achieved his Geshe Degree, the equivalent in the West of a doctorate.

He teaches in the Yungdrung Bon and other Buddhist traditions, and is a qualified Rimé teacher, which means "non-sectarian" in Tibetan.

His spiritual training has developed in him an extraordinary depth of knowledge through which he clearly conveys essential teachings and their meaning. He has authored nine books in Tibetan on Tibetan culture, history and religion, and has presented at numerous conferences in Asia, Europe and the U.S. He came to California in 2013 to instruct Western Students. He founded Kunsang Gar Center, of which he is currently the spiritual director and teacher.